Cover illustration Messerschmitt 109s of Ist Gruppe Lehrgeschwader 1.

1 A Messerschmitt 109F of III./JG 26 returning to its base at Liegescourt in Northern France, summer 1941. (Schoepfel)

WARBIRDS ILLUSTRATED NO. 1

The LUFTWAFFE
1933-1945

Volume I   ALFRED PRICE

ARMS AND ARMOUR PRESS
London—Melbourne—Harrisburg, Pa.

Introduction

This book is the first in a series by Arms and Armour Press, and depicts various aspects of the Luftwaffe between 1933 and 1945. The majority of the photographs have come from private collections, picked up during numerous research visits to Germany. I tender my grateful thanks to the many kind gentlemen who generously allowed me to make copies of the photographs in their albums. In each case, the photographs have been selected for their interest to the enthusiast, the historian and the modeller; I have made no attempt to follow any cohesive historical theme. Further volumes in this series will follow in due course, and I trust the reader will find them of similar interest.

Alfred Price, 1981.

Warbird 1: The Luftwaffe, 1933–1945, Volume I
Published in 1981 by
Arms and Armour Press, Lionel Leventhal Limited,
2–6 Hampstead High Street, London NW3 1QQ;
4–12 Tattersalls Lane, Melbourne, Victoria 3000, Australia;
Cameron and Kelker Streets, P.O. Box 1831, Harrisburg, Pennsylvania 17105, U.S.A.

British Library Cataloguing in Publication Data:
The Luftwaffe, 1933–1945.—(Warbirds illustrated)
1
1. Germany—Luftwaffe—History
I. Title   II. Price, Alfred   III. Series
358.4'00943   D787
ISBN 0-85368-218-6

Layout by Anthony A. Evans.
Printed in Great Britain by William Clowes, Beccles, Limited.

◀ **2** A Ju 88 of KG 76 returning to its base in East Prussia.

3 Junkers 52 bombers passing low over the Nuremberg stadium during one of the pre-war Nazi Party rallies. (via Bode)

4 Ju 52 bombers of Ist Gruppe of KG 152 during a formation exercise before the war. Note the 'dustbin' ventral gun position in its lowered position under the fuselage of the aircraft in the foreground. (via Schliephake)

5 Officers and men of KG 152 parading past Field Marshal von Blomberg at Neubranden-burg in 1936, after the formation of the unit. KG 152 was re-numbered KG 1 in August 1939. (Wilhelm)

6, 7 Heinkel 51 fighters of Jagdgeschwader 132 'Richthofen' at their airfield at Jueterbog-Damm in 1935. (via Schliephake)

The Junkers 86 bomber entered service in 1936, a status few diesel-powered aircraft achieved. **8** A Geschwader formation of Ju 86s; 67 aircraft are visible in the photograph. **9** Ju 86s of KG 253 photographed during aerial manoeuvres early in 1937.

▲6 ▼7

▲8   ▼9

▲10 ▼11

10 Waiting for the war to begin: Junkers 87s of Ist Gruppe StG 77, and a Fieseler 156, at the forward base at Neudorf near Oppeln in Silesia, late in August 1939. **11** Ju 87s of I./StG 77 about to take off for their first operational missions, against Polish positions on 1 September 1939. (Scheffel)
12 The view from the gunner's position in a Ju 87 of I./StG 77 after it had pulled out of its dive following an attack on the suburbs of Warsaw early in September 1939. **13** Damage inflicted by ground fire on the Ju 87 flown by Oberleutnant Hartmann of I./StG 77 during an attack on Polish positions on 6 September 1939. (Scheffel)

▲14 ▼15

14 Heinkel 111 bombers of Kampfgruppe 100 between missions during the Norwegian campaign, at their base at Trondheim/Vaernes in the late spring of 1940. Although it was trained to carry out precision night attacks using the X-Gerät equipment, the unit operated in the normal day-bombing rôle over Norway. **15** Unteroffizier Horst Goetz of KGr 100 in his He 111; the aircraft carries the unit's 'viking ship' badge. (Goetz)

16 Messerschmitt 109Es of III./JG 26, believed to have been photographed at Villa-coublay near Paris in June 1940. Note that the aircraft nearest the camera, and the one third in the line, have had their fuselage markings partially sprayed over; this may have been done when extending the light blue undersurfaces higher up the fuselage. (Schoepfel)

17 Messerschmitt 109s of 6./JG 27 dispersed at the side of their airfield at St. Trond in Belgium in May 1940 during the campaign in the west. (Neumann)

▲16 ▼17

▲18

▲19

18 Dornier 17s of 9./KG 76 in formation over France.
19 An abandoned R.A.F. Hurricane being inspected by German aircrew at Beauvais, home of I./KG 76 during the Battle of Britain. (Rehm)
20, 21 Dornier 17s of II./KG 2 photographed over England during the Battle of Britain. (Borner)

◀20 ▼21

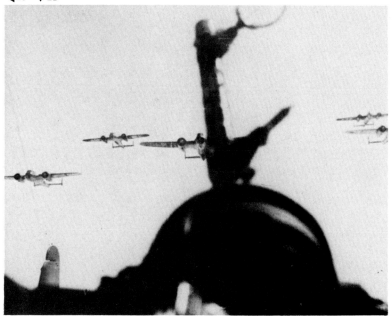

▲ 22 ▼ 23

Scenes at the forward airfield of Augot, Normandy, home of I./StG 77, during the Battle of Britain. **22** A Ju 87 being manhandled to its dispersal point. **23** A dive-bomber which has 'nosed over' on soft ground to become an 'airman's memorial'; an unusual feature of this aircraft is that the individual identification letter has been painted outside the markings on the top of each wing. (Scheffel)

24 A Staffel formation of Heinkel 111s of Kampfgeschwader 55, taken during September 1940.

▲25 ▼26

▲27

▲28 ▼29

25 A pair of Messerschmitt 110s of I./ZG 52. In June 1940 this unit was re-numbered II./ZG 2.

26 A Messerschmitt 110 of I./ZG 2.

27–29 Close-up shots of SC 250 bombs – 250kg Spreng Cylindrische or general purpose weapons – about to be loaded onto Ju 87s. Note that these bombs have knobs protruding from the sides of their bodies. The purpose of these was to engage the fork mechanism which would swing them clear of the propeller when they were released in the dive.

▲30

30 Dornier 17s of KG 76 photographed during the Battle of Britain. **31** This is not a very clear shot but one of great interest. It was taken at about 1pm on 16 August 1940, from the Do 17 of 9./KG 76 piloted by Unteroffizier Günther Unger, and shows a squadron of ten Hurricanes climbing into position to attack. The unit was probably No. 111 Squadron, which attacked the Dorniers from head-on shortly afterwards. One of the Hurricanes, piloted by Flight Lieutenant Henry Ferris, collided with the Do 17 of Oberfeldwebel Edmund Riedel and both aircraft crashed near Marden. There were no survivors from either machine. (Rehm, Unger)

▼31

▲32 ▼33

32 A well-known photograph of a Dornier 17 shot down during the Battle of Britain, which has appeared with various captions (and variously aligned!). It was in fact an aircraft of I./KG 76, which was shot down by Pilot Officer Alan Eckford in a Hurricane of No. 32 Squadron and crashed at Hurst Green near Oxted in Surrey early on the afternoon of 18 August. **33** Feldwebel Wilhelm Lautersack was one of the two crewmen who managed to bail out of the plunging bomber before it struck the ground. (Lautersack)

21

▲34 ▼35

Scenes at the fighter airfield at Caffiers near Calais, home of III./JG 26 during the Battle of Britain. These photographs are from the album of fighter ace Gerhard Schoepfel, who then held the rank of Hauptmann. **34** The unit's senior officers discussing an operation outside the temporary headquarters of the Gruppe. Seated on the left is Schoepfel, with the Gruppe commander, Major (as he was then) Adolf Galland, to his immediate right. **35** Pilots of III./JG 26 pictured during the Battle of Britain: left to right, Leutnant Lüdewig, Leutnant Heinz Ebeling, Schoepfel, Oberleutnant Josef Haiböck and Leutnant Hans Nauman. **36** Ground crewmen changing the engine of a Messerschmitt 109. **37** Building a sandbag blast pen for a single fighter. (Schoepfel)

▲38 ▼39

38 Gerhard Schoepfel in his fighter. **39** The victory bars on the tail of Schoepfel's Messerschmitt on the evening of 18 August 1940, showing those for the four Hurricanes of No. 501 Squadron he shot down that day. (Schoepfel) **40** Aircraft of III./JG 26 in their camouflaged dispersals at Caffiers. **41** A Messerschmitt 109E of III./JG 26 loaded with an SC 250 bomb about to take-off for an attack on Britain during the closing stages of the Battle of Britain. (Schoepfel)

▲43

Photographs taken at Catania, Sicily, in April 1941 as the Messerschmitt 109Es of I./JG 27 were preparing to move to Libya.
42 (on previous spread) Ground crewmen holding down the tail of Oberleutnant Ludwig Franzisket's Messerschmitt as the engine is warmed up; note the drop tank under the fuselage.
43 Hauptmann Karl-Wolfgang Redlich (left foreground, with papers) during the briefing of his pilots. The two men in flying kit in the foreground were the crew of a Messerschmitt 110 which was to lead the formation across the Mediterranean. Note

the early type tropical filter on the supercharger air intake of the aircraft in the immediate background. (Schroer)

44 Messerschmitt 109s of I./JG 27 dispersed at their landing ground at Gambut in Libya soon after their arrival. The photograph gives a good impression of the primitive conditions under which the fighters had to operate. **45** Major Edouard Neumann, the commander of I./JG 27, pictured wearing the makeshift 'uniform' he used in North Africa, a mixture of items of German and Italian kit. (Schroer, Neumann)

▼44

45▶

46, 47 Ju 87s of I./StG 77 photographed at Prilep in Yugoslavia during the Balkans campaign. (Schmidt, Scheffel) **48** A Ju 87 of I./StG 77 returning from an operation, the bomb fork mechanism swinging freely in the slipstream. **49** An old Junkers G 38 transport operated by KGr.zbV 172 during the Balkans campaign; this aircraft was destroyed during an R.A.F. attack on Athens in May 1941. (Schmidt)

▲46 ▼47

▲50 ▼51

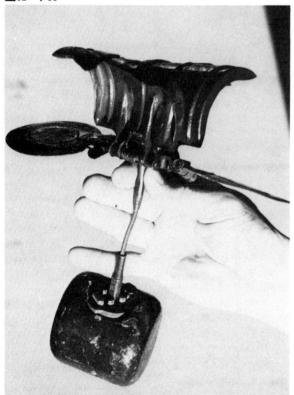

Junkers 87 dive-bombers of I./StG 2 attacking bridges north of Novgorod on 17 August 1941. **50** Aircraft pulling away after scoring a direct hit on a railway bridge. **51** A hit or a very near miss on a road bridge.

52 A Heinkel 111 of KGr 126 which had a lucky escape after it was rammed by a Soviet fighter. Note the propeller slashes at the top of the fin and the damage to the rear of the starboard engine nacelle.

53 The SD-2, a 2kg weapon known in Britain as the 'Butterfly Bomb', was used in large numbers during the early part of the campaign in Russia. **54** SD-2s bursting across an airfield during an attack by Ju 88s of KG 51. (Price, Dierich)

55 A close shave for a Condor crew. This aircraft ran into a 'parachute and cable' device fired from a British ship it was attacking. The device was fired vertically from the ship and comprised a parachute and a long length of cable, on the end of which was a small bomb; if an aircraft's wing struck the cable, the parachute would draw the bomb up to the wing where it would detonate. Fortunately for the German crew, on this occasion the parachute did not open until the container hit the ground as the Condor was landing at Merignac. **56** Men of I./KG 40 examining the unusual weapon; on the right, wearing a peaked cap, is Hauptmann Bernhard Jope. (Jope)

57, 58 Armourers loading SC 250 bombs on Heinkel 111s of KG 55.

▲ 57 ▼ 58

▲59 ▼60

59 Dornier 17s of III./KG 2.
60 Ground crewmen replacing the engine covers on a Heinkel 111 of I./KG 26.

The Condor in detail. **61** The HDL 151 hydraulically-operated turret, carrying either an MG 151 15mm or 20mm gun, was fitted in the forward upper positions of most Condors of the C-3 and later versions. **62** A single MG 15 7.9mm machine-gun, which was fired from the side of the rear fuselage of the Condor. The leather bag under the drum magazine was to collect the spent cartridge cases. **63** Inside the Condor during a maritime reconnaissance mission; note the large fuel tank installed in the fuselage. (Jope, via Selinger)

▲61

▲62 ▼63

▲66

▲67

64 (on previous spread) An
early type Focke Wulf 200
Condor of I./KG 40 photo-
graphed over the Atlantic. 65
Aircraft and crews of I./KG 40
lined up for inspection at
Bordeaux/Merignac in July
1941. (Kowalewski)
66, 67 Ground crewmen
loading up SC 250s on to FW
200s of I./KG 40 at Bordeaux/
Merignac. Note the use of
wooden blocks to enable the
hydraulic lifting trolleys to get
the bombs high enough for
them to fit on the shackles in
the recesses under the outer
engines. The top photograph
(66) shows an aircraft bearing
the 'world in a ring' emblem of
KG 40 and the name 'Mars' on
the nose; its fuselage bomb
doors are open. (Kowalewski,
Jope)

◄65

▲68 ▼69

68 A Junkers 87 specially modified for deck-landing operations; note the hook in front of the tail wheel. The aircraft is seen here crossing the Alps in the winter of 1942 on its way to Italy for trials with the electrical arrester gear developed for the Italian aircraft-carrier *Aquila*. **69** A Junkers 88C fighter of III./KG 76 at Catania, Sicily, May 1943. This aircraft was flown by Hauptmann Diether Lukesch on strafing operations against Allied airfields in North Africa. (Bode, Lukesch)

70, 71 Arado 196 seaplanes of 4. Staffel Bordflieger Gruppe 196, operating in the Adriatic area late in 1943. This type of aircraft was used for short-range anti-submarine and shipping protection patrols. (via Rigglesford)

▲70 ▼71

▲72 ▼73

Heinkel 111 bombers of I./KG 100 operating on the southern part of the Russian front in the summer of 1943. **72, 73** Aircraft parked beside the open bomb dump. The SC 50 and SC 250 bombs, many of them fitted with cardboard screamers on the fins, await loading. (Bätcher)
74, 75 Heinkel 111s of I./KG 100.

76 The heaviest type of free-fall bomb carried in action by the Luftwaffe was the SC 2500 'Max', seen here about to be loaded on the external rack of an He 111 of KG 100. 77 The nose of an He 111 of KG 100 fitted with an MG FF 20mm cannon. The wreath on the end of the cannon was put there during celebrations to mark the 500th operational mission by Major Hans-Georg Bätcher, the commander of I./KG 100. (Bätcher)

▲76 ▼77

78 Ground crewmen adjusting SC 250 bombs fitted on the external racks of an He 111 of KG 100; note the cardboard screamers fitted to the fins. **79** A special weapon for burning wooden bridges, devised by Hans-Georg Bätcher. It comprised the nose and tail assemblies of a normal SC 1000 bomb, sandwiched between which were two oil drums filled with cotton waste, oil and petrol. The whole assemblage was welded together, strengthening bars were fitted and a pair of incendiary bombs were mounted on the side. On hitting the water up-stream of the bridge, the bomb broke up, spilling out the inflammable filling which was ignited by the incendiary bombs. The blazing mass was then to drift down to the bridge and set it alight. The weapon was successful on a few occasions. (Bätcher)

▲ 78   ▼ 79

▲80 ▼81

▲82 ▼83

Attempt to fool. **80** The Luftwaffe airfield at Nordholz near Cuxhaven, showing the characteristic triangular pattern of runways and the 'ladder' parking area, all toned down with paint to make them as inconspicuous as possible from above. **81** A decoy airfield 4 miles away, near Holssel, which has the same features but brightly painted to appear conspicuous from the air.

Rocket firing single-engined fighters used against U.S. heavy bombers in 1943. **82** A Messerschmitt 109G of II./JG 11 flown by Oberleutnant Heinz Knoke. **83** A 21cm rocket in its launching tube under the wing of an FW 190. (Knoke, via Creek)

84 A close-up of the nose of an Me 410 of ZG 1 in the spring of 1944. This version of the bomber destroyer carried two MG 151 20mm cannon in the lower part of the nose, two more in the under-fuselage tray, and four 13mm heavy machine-guns across the centre of the nose. Note the 'wasp' emblem of the Geschwader. (via Redemann)
Long-range armament alternatives on the Me 410 bomber destroyer. **85** A pair of 21cm rocket-launchers under the outer wing sections. **86** A 5cm BK 5 high-velocity cannon which fired shells weighing 1.6kg (3½lb) with a muzzle velocity of 920m/sec (2,800ft/sec); note the telescopic sight fitted into the windscreen. (Stehle, Bucholz)

◄84   ▲85 ▼86

▲87 ▼88

87–89 Me 410 bomber destroyers of II./ZG 26, based at Königsberg/Neumark in the spring and summer of 1944, which used the BK 5 cannon in action against U.S. heavy bombers. **90** Feldwebel Fritz Bucholz of II./ZG 26 in his Me 410, wearing his steel flying helmet. (Bucholz, Stehle)

▲89 ▼90

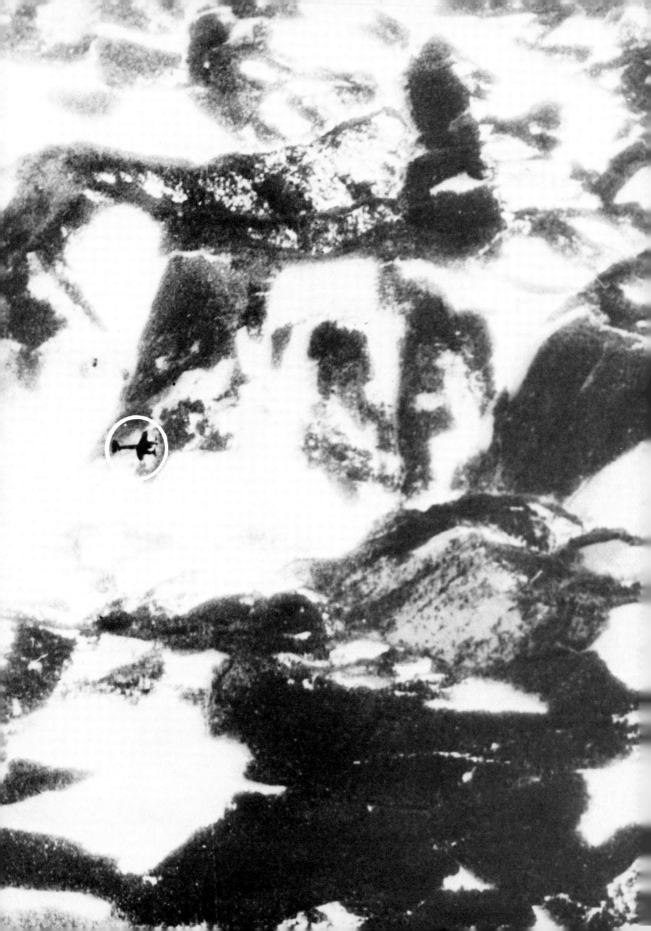

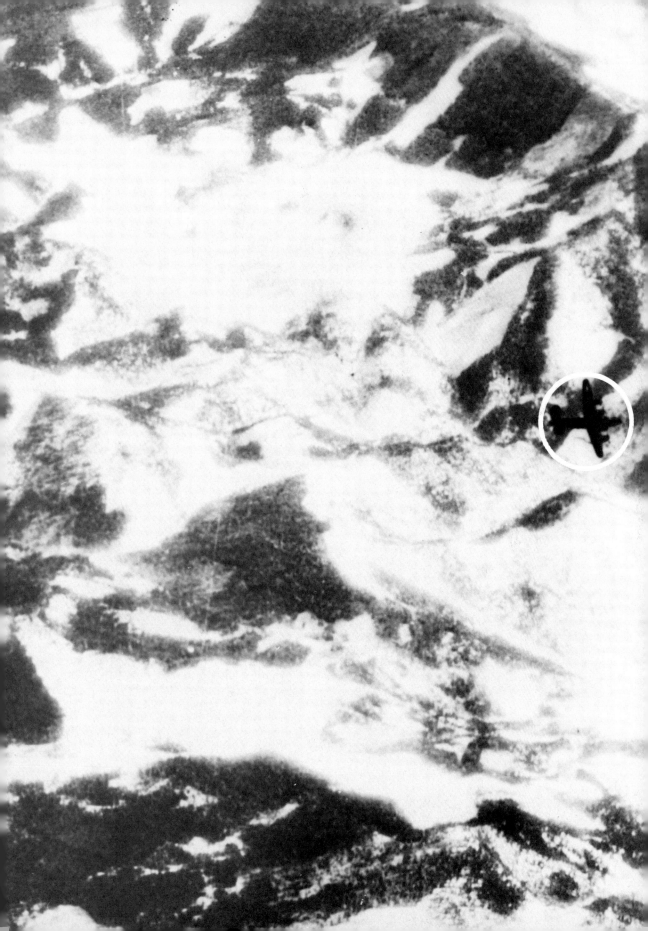

▲92 ▼93   ▼94

91 (on previous spread) The snow-covered Alps form a deceptively beautiful backdrop as an Me 410 of II./ZG 26 sits about 350 yards behind a B-24 and finishes it off, following the U.S. 15th Air Force attack on Steyr in Austria, on 23 February 1944. (U.S.A.F.)

The Luftwaffe made large-scale use of 'Sturm' tactics from the spring of 1944, employing specially heavily armoured FW 190s which made massed attacks from short range against U.S. heavy bomber formations. **92** Three of the most famous 'Sturm' pilots: from right to left, Oberst Walther Dahl, who was a leading exponent of these methods; Hauptmann Wilhelm Möritz of IV. (Sturm)/JG 3; and Leutnant Oskar Romm, also of this unit. **93** Oberfeldwebel Walter Loos, who flew for a time with IV. (Sturm)/JG 3, was credited with a total of 22 four-engined bombers shot down. He himself was shot down a total of nine times, but survived the war. **94** Feldwebel Hans Schäfer of IV./(Sturm) JG 3, wearing on his flying jacket the 'whites of the eyes' insignia which distinguished the Sturm-gruppe pilots. (Romm, Loos, Schäfer)

95, 96 Heavily armoured FW 190A-8s of II. (Sturm)/JG 300 photographed at their base at Loebnitz towards the end of 1944. These aircraft were each fitted with a pair of the devastatingly effective MK 108 30mm cannon, just outboard of the undercarriage legs. (Schröder)

▲95 ▼96

▲ 97

97 The low-velocity MK 108 cannon, with one of its 30mm high-explosive shells. The cannon fired 330gr (11½oz) rounds with a muzzle velocity of 540m/sec (1,750ft/sec) at a rate of 660 per minute. **98** This B-17 Fortress of the 457th Bomb Group was lucky to regain its base in Britain after being shot-up by German fighters. The damage to the port wing is consistent with hits from one or two 30mm explosive rounds; on average, three hits with such rounds were sufficient to knock down a heavy bomber. (Price, U.S.A.F.)

99, 100 Secret weapon: an FW 190 carrying a pair of test rounds of the Ruhrstahl X-4 air-to-air guided missile. Powered by a liquid fuel rocket motor, the X-4 was steered at its target by command signals transmitted down thin wires unreeled from the weapon. The X-4 weighed about 60kg (133lb) at launch, of which 20kg (44lb) was warhead; the maximum effective range was about 3,000 metres.

▼ 98

▲101 ▼102

Heinkel 162 fighters of Jagdgeschwader 1 lined up at Leck in Schleswig-Holstein in May 1945, waiting to surrender to the advancing British ground forces. **101** The commander of I. Gruppe, Oberleutnant Emil Demuth, with his personal He 162. The 16 victory bars were a carry over of Demuth's score while flying FW 190s; it is believed the He 162 never fired its guns in anger. **102** Hauptmann Küniger of 3. Staffel, with his personal aircraft. **103, 104** He 162s drawn up at Leck. **105** Pilots of JG 1 who flew the He 162: left to right, Major Zober, Oberst Herbert Ihlefeld, the commander of the Geschwader, Hauptmann Küniger, Demuth, unknown, unknown, Hauptmann Gerhard Strasen and (partially concealed) Hauptmann Ludewig. (Demuth)

▲103

▲104 ▼105

▲106

▲107 ▼108

The He 162 in close-up. **106, 107** The nose of the aircraft, showing detail of the cockpit, gunsight, port for the MG 151 20mm cannon, and the nose wheel assembly. **108** The anhedral section on the port wing-tip, to improve lateral stability. **109** The rear fuselage, showing the 'acorn' fairing at the rear of the BMW 003 jet engine. Prior to take-off its extension had to be checked against the white marks painted below it; the extension at the trailing edge of the wing root, downwards, was a modification to reduce buffeting. **110** A close-up of the fin and rudder assembly.

120086

▲111 ▼112

111, 112 An He 162 which made a wheels-up landing during a training flight. The weakness of the light plywood and metal structure is evident. (Demuth)
113 An He 162 comes in to land at Leck with flaps down.
114 An He 162 in French markings, undergoing testing at Mont de Marsan in France in 1946. (via Marchand)

▲113 ▼114

▲115

115, 116 Another type which appeared just too late to see operational service was the Dornier 335 push-pull fighter. The version depicted above (**116**) was the V 14, the prototype of the B version for the bomber destroyer rôle which had an MK 103 high-velocity 30mm cannon in each wing. (via Selinger)
117 The two-seater Do 335A-12, which was built as an operational conversion trainer for the push-pull fighter.

118, 119 The end: Messerschmitt 110G night fighters of III./NJG 1 photographed at Fritzlar shortly after the airfield had been overrun by the U.S. Third Army. Some of the aircraft had been blown up by the retreating Germans, others had their port main wheel tyres shot through by American troops to prevent unauthorized flights. (U.S.A.F.)